Cryptocurrency for Beginners

A Guide to Learn About The Blockchain, Mining, Wallets, and Investing in Bitcoin, Ethereum, Litecoin, & More

Table of Contents

Introduction 1

Chapter 1: Introduction to the Main Concepts 3
    Distributed Ledger Technology 3
    Blockchain Technology 8
    How a Blockchain Works 9

Chapter 2: Overview of Cryptocurrencies 11
    Definition 12
    History 12
    The Popular Cryptocurrencies 15
    The Top 10 Cryptocurrencies 15
    Ethereum Smart Contract 20
    DAO and DAPP 22

Chapter 3: Investing in Cryptocurrencies 25
    Cryptocurrency Market Capitalization 25
    What is Market Capitalization? 26
    How to Invest in Cryptocurrency 27
    Cryptocurrency Wallets 29
    Types of Cryptocurrency Wallets 29
    The Best Wallet Option for Aspiring Cryptocurrency Investors 31
    How to Invest in Cryptocurrencies 33
    A few things to keep in mind 35

Chapter 4: Mining Cryptocurrencies 37

    Definition 37

    Bitcoin Mining 37

    Breaking Down the Basics of Bitcoin Mining 38

    The Role of Bitcoin Miners 39

    The Bitcoin Mining Process 39

    Advancements in Bitcoin Mining 42

    How to get involved in Bitcoin Mining 45

    What is a Mining Pool? 45

    Ethereum Mining 47

Conclusion 51

Introduction

You no doubt must have come across the term Cryptocurrency before now, arguably the most popular emerging technology in the world today. The internet is replete with numerous articles and blog posts of several matters relating to the world of Cryptocurrencies and how they are shaping the global financial landscape.

When Satoshi Nakamoto, the unknown person (or group of persons) who released the White Paper on Bitcoin as a Peer-to-Peer payment processing solution in 2008, few could have anticipated the sweeping impact the technology would have across the globe. Bitcoin was the beginning of the revolution and since then, other Cryptocurrency variants have been introduced with varying degrees of success and market penetration.

While Cryptocurrencies might have initially been envisaged as a means of achieving secure payment processing, the underlying technology behind it (Blockchain Technology) has been put to many uses. The introduction of the Ethereum Blockchain and its use of Smart Contracts have shown many stakeholders in the field that the potential applications of Cryptocurrencies and Blockchain Technology are limitless. These days, the technology is being applied by Governments and Large Corporations alike.

The purpose of this book is to educate beginners on how to go about investing in Cryptocurrencies. As at the time of writing this book, the total market capitalization of Cryptocurrencies stands at $170 billion. If this figure does not impress you, consider that at the start of the year, the market cap stood at $17.7 billion. This means that in a little over half a year, Cryptocurrencies have experienced a market cap growth of more than 850%. No other tradable asset has ever seen such growth.

With such astounding figures and growth potential, investing in the market is a wise decision. With numerous ICOs (Initial Coin Offerings) scheduled for release in the coming months and the rapid rise in adoption of Cryptocurrencies, the market is only going to get bigger. This is not a bubble, but rather, the next big market explosion just like the way technology start-ups was, a few years ago.

In order to successfully invest in Cryptocurrencies, you need not just information, but the right sort. This book is designed to present even the least knowledgeable person in the Cryptocurrency space with practical knowledge that will help them on their way to successfully navigating the Cryptocurrency Investment scene. Great care has been taken to ensure that technical aspects of Cryptocurrencies are explained in everyday easy to understand language.

Chapter 1
Introduction to the Main Concepts

Cryptocurrencies are based on a collection of concept technologies that allow them to function the way they do. At the heart of cryptocurrency functionality are Cryptography, Distributed Ledger technology (DLT) and Blockchain Technology. The history of Cryptocurrencies can be thought to be like a chapter in the history of Cryptography itself, with DLT and Blockchain being the mechanism by which Cryptographic technology has been appropriated to payment systems. Before delving into the main portion of this book which deals with Cryptocurrencies, it is important to briefly examine DLT and Blockchain Technology in order to provide a context that will aid better understanding of the core subject matter of this book.

Distributed Ledger Technology

You might be familiar with what a ledger is, a record of transactions, usually showing debit and credit amounts. Ledgers go back many centuries having been used in business activities over the ages. In its simplest form, a ledger contains information about a particular transaction in terms of whether it is a debit or credit transaction (payment being made or payment being received) as well as other details like date and name of the transaction in question.

An important aspect of the business activity is proper record keeping. Ledgers are basically, record documents of the transactions carried out by a particular business enterprise. In the 21st-century world, the business space has become ever more global and with the internet, it has become possible for integrated business networks to emerge. These integrated business networks combine together to form a global marketplace where all stakeholders participate in the transfer of assets. This is where ledgers come into play. A transaction is simply a transfer of value in the form of assets from one party to another. This transfer is then recorded in a document known as a ledger. For many typical businesses the world over, many different ledgers will be maintained containing information on all the many transactions carried out by the business.

Ledgers like all other System of Records (SORs) in use in the world today have a number of flaws inherent in them. One of the biggest challenges in business today, especially with the transfer of value operations is the **"Cost of Trust"**. The cost of trust basically refers to the cost incurred in order to validate and authenticate a transaction. Consider a typical online payment that requires you entering your credit card details and having a third-party payment processor validate the payment. Both the merchant and the buyer are depending on the third-party payment processor to ensure the fidelity of the transaction. This dependence is manifested in the form of transaction processing fees paid to these third-party payment processors. All mainstream business transactions require validation from a "reputable" third-party. What happens when these so-called reputable third-parties make mistakes or decide to manipulate figures? How do we checkmate the occurrence of such things?

The general idea behind a Distributed Ledger is based on the many deficiencies that plague the business ledgers in use today. There is a lack of transparency and the likelihood of fraud and manipulation because transactions are being authorized by centralized financial institutions. There is also the fact that having to require these centralized authorizing and authenticating bodies leads to the occurrence of a lot of transaction bottlenecks brought about by slow processing activities. Imagine not being able to push through a vital transaction in time simply because the clearinghouse couldn't process the transaction quickly enough. Many business deals have been thwarted because of this very reason. As a consequence of not wanting to have transactions delayed, there has in recent years been the emergence of tiered transactions, i.e. transactions being given a hierarchical order of importance which isn't in the spirit of fair business practices.

Furthermore, in the event of disputes between the parties to any transaction, the process of resolution represents a considerable cost burden on both parties. This is in addition to the previously stated transaction fees. All of these contribute to making many business dealings unnecessarily expensive. There is also the occurrence of ledgers having discrepancies on both or either side of the transaction. This leads to delays which can hamper normal business function as it is generally unwise to base decisions on an unverified ledger since the information it contains isn't yet up-to-date. A lot of time, effort and resources are expended during the reconciliation process, i.e. trying to make sure the ledgers of both parties agree. This then brings up the need for auditing procedures which in themselves are another addition to the cost implications of the transaction.

The idea behind the emergence of the DLT was based upon the need to solve these aforementioned problems. The fundamental ideas behind DLT are a mutually shared decentralized ledger that required less reconciliation due to protocols set in place to automatically authenticate and validate each transaction in a matter of a few seconds to a few minutes. Let's try to break this down.

- Mutually Shared Ledger

    In the mainstream business space, each entity maintains its own ledger. So if entity A and entity B decide to carry out a transaction, each will have to update their own ledger when the transaction is completely based on the authentication and authorization provided by the necessary third-party (banks, brokers, clearing houses etc.). In the distributed ledger framework, there are no single ledgers for each entity; instead, there is a shared ledger that is distributed amongst the participants of the business network. This mutually shared ledger is updated as soon as each transaction has been verified by a majority consensus within the network. Thus, verification is no longer the responsibility of a single central third-party institution; rather it becomes the responsibility of every participant in the network.

Introduction to the Main Concepts

This network within which the ledger is distributed is what is referred to as a **Blockchain**. Blockchains will be discussed in subsequent sections of this chapter. With the decentralized ledger being distributed across the network of participants, there is no longer any need for tedious reconciliation process with additional cost implications. The rules embedded into the network protocols allow for the reconciliation process to be automated and free from manipulation and mistakes. By introducing an incentive-based transaction validation process, the integrity of the network is maintained within the boundaries of a theoretically immutable system. This incentive-based transaction validation process is what is known as Cryptocurrency Mining which is discussed in detail in Chapter 4 of this book.

- Cryptography

No serious business wants to have all of its financial information floating around in cyberspace. Security is an important component of all business transaction and this is one of the core service provided by financial institutions; anonymity. If there is going to be a shared ledger that is accessible to every member of the network, some security infrastructure has to be put in place to prevent one user from manipulating or gaining access to the data of another user. There is where cryptography comes into play. By means of **public key cryptography**, each user can encrypt their transactions and only the intended participant can gain access to the data. This adds an extra layer of security within the DLT framework.

Blockchain Technology

Blockchain Technology represents the first successful implementation of the DLT framework and while there are more of such implementations being developed, there is no denying that they will have to be extra special in order to knock the blockchain off its perch.

Definition

A Blockchain is essentially a network of computing nodes having the same copies of a mutually shared database (distributed ledger) in which updates and changes to the records stored in the database are made by means of a majority consensus based upon some predefined mathematical rules. Each transaction forms a **"block"** which is linked to other transaction blocks forming the *blockchain*. In its most basic form, a blockchain can be imagined to be an infinitely long chain made up of transaction blocks all the way down to the first transaction block in the chain known as the **Genesis Block**. As usual, let us break down this seemingly complex definition.

It begins with understanding what a network is. When two or more computers share information with one another, a network is formed. In the blockchain network, the information being shared is the single mutually distributed ledger which is replicated and shared to all the participating network nodes (computers).

When a new computer connects to the blockchain, it sends a request to the nearest available node (peer) in order to gain access to the distributed ledger. Depending on the protocols set up within the blockchain network, there are numerous types of nodes present in a blockchain network. There are nodes that maintain a full copy of the distributed ledger, there are others that hold an abridged copy and there are some solely responsible for validating transactions. These last group of nodes are called mining nodes and will be explained in greater detail in chapter 4 of this book.

How a Blockchain Works

Blockchains run on decentralized peer-to-peer (P2P) networks with no central server. What exists is a vast network of computing nodes all communicating with each other and maintaining the network. Each node in the network has two addresses; a public key and a private key. Think of these like your credit card number and your CVV number. These addresses are used for initiating and finalizing transactions within the network.

When a transaction is to be carried out between participant A and participant B in the network, they make use of the cryptocurrency running on the blockchain. Let us assume that A wishes to make a purchase from B. A will initiate a transfer of a certain amount of **"coins"** (the colloquial term for cryptocurrencies) to the public address of B. This transaction request will be broadcasted to the entire network and mining nodes will attempt to validate the authenticity of this transaction by means of some complex mathematical proofs. Once validated, the transaction becomes a "block" and it is added to the blockchain. Participant B then receives the specified amount of coins and the transaction is complete. In this way, payment is processed without the need for third-party authentication thereby cutting out unnecessary delays and extra fees.

There have been a number of advancements in the mathematical proofs used by different blockchain networks. When Satoshi Nakamoto introduced Bitcoin, the proof mechanism utilized was called the "proof-of-work" and it eliminated the double-spend problem which had been the one criticism of decentralized payment systems prior to bitcoins. In the years that have followed, other iterations of mathematical proofs have been introduced in different blockchain networks such as "proof-of-stake" and "proof-of-burn" just to mention a few. These will be explained in chapter 4 of this book when cryptocurrency mining is discussed in detail.

Chapter 2
Overview of Cryptocurrencies

There are many who believe Cryptocurrencies to be the future of the money and it isn't particularly hard to see why. Despite the fact that cryptocurrencies haven't yet become recognized as currency by many Governments, the rate of adoption by millions of people around the world are clear indicators of the potential that cryptocurrencies have. The allure of a decentralized currency not being controlled by Governments and Central Banks is one which seems to appeal to a lot of people and who can blame them. The financial institutions of the day haven't exactly acquitted themselves most honorably as history has been able to show countless times.

Cryptocurrencies open an entirely new vista of limitless opportunities that will allow a greater number of people access to the global financial marketplace. With seamless transaction protocols and superfast authentication and authorization processes, cryptocurrencies provide a payment processing platform that is bound to launch humanity into a more advanced global economic system. The current economic setup of the world today disenfranchises a great number of people, generally referred to an "unbankable." These people have limited access to financial services due to the certain rules and regulations that preclude them from being able to participate. However, within the cryptocurrency space, the only limitation to one's ability to participate will be access to technology.

Definition

Cryptocurrency quite literally means "cryptographic currency", i.e. currency based upon cryptographic technology (encryption). Cryptocurrencies are decentralized digital currencies that are backed up by Blockchain Technology. They do not require a third-party intermediary in order for them to be used in performing financial transactions as all validation protocols are embedded within the Blockchain framework on which the cryptocurrency runs. Cryptographic encryption is used as the mechanism by which transactions are secured and additional units of the cryptocurrency are created.

What this means is that when using cryptocurrencies to pay for items online, for example, you do not need a payment processor like MasterCard or Visa to validate your transaction. As long as you have the required coins (colloquial term for cryptocurrency), the transaction will proceed.

History

It is common for most experts in the field of cryptocurrency when attempting to give a history of cryptocurrency to split the study into two different epochs: the pre-Bitcoin and post-Bitcoin era. While it might seem to the uninitiated that there weren't any cryptocurrency variants before bitcoin, the reality, however, is the exact opposite.

The Pre-Bitcoin Era

Before Satoshi Nakamoto, the unknown pioneer of Bitcoin released the now famous White Paper introducing Bitcoin to the world, there had been several attempts to create an internet-based digital currency. The general working idea was hinged around a form of currency that was immune to the imperfections in fiat currency, a way of restoring the "integrity" of money. Many individuals had become dissatisfied with Governments and mainstream Financial Institutions.

Numerous attempts have been made over the years to create electronic money systems. In 1983, David Chaum invented the "blinding formula", an improvement on the basic RSA algorithm still being used in many web encryption protocols today. This then led to the creation of DigiCash, an e-cash solution framework developed in the Netherlands. Due to a combination of poor business practices and an inability to honor its agreement with the DNB (the Central Bank of the Netherlands), DigiCash went bankrupt in 1998.

By the late 90s, an increase in the number of electronic payment options being developed due to rapid advancements in internet technology led to many digital cash solutions being created. Perhaps the most popular of them all was e-gold, the "bitcoin of the early to mid-2000s". Based out of Nevis in the Caribbean, e-gold was digital currency backed up by gold that enjoyed massive success in the few years of its existence. Due to stringent post 9/11 regulatory measures adopted in the United States over concerns that cryptocurrencies were being used by unsavory individuals (terrorists, drug dealers etc.), e-gold was shut down in 2005 and signaled the end of its operations.

The Post-Bitcoin Era

In 2008, two fundamentally important events happened in the global financial scene. One was the global financial meltdown and the other was Satoshi Nakamoto's White Paper as a blockchain based Peer-to-Peer payment processing system. In fact, some stakeholders posit that the global financial crisis of 2008 was a contributing factor to the way and manner in which Bitcoin and other cryptocurrencies that followed gained such a wide acceptance.

Prior to Nakamoto's White Paper, the major problem facing the implementation of cryptocurrencies was the problem of "double-spending." Double spending refers to spending the same money twice and prior to Bitcoin, was the major bane of digital monetary systems (cryptocurrencies). The Bitcoin White Paper introduced an ingenious way to deal with this problem by means of an immutable Blockchain with a mutually shared distributed ledger. This meant that the same coins could not be spent twice.

With this problem solved, it was open season for cryptocurrency developers all over the world with many different Blockchains being created subsequently. In 2014, developer Vitalik Buterin created Ethereum, a more complex and superior Blockchain Technology than Bitcoin with increased functionality and applicability. Today, there are more than 900 different cryptocurrencies in use and this number is expected to keep on growing.

The Popular Cryptocurrencies

Since the introduction of Bitcoin, there have been numerous other cryptocurrencies that have emerged. However, not all of them have introduced any meaningful technological update to the cryptocurrency space. Most of these cryptocurrencies are for payment processing but there have been a few coins that have been created to service non-financial transactions in areas such as music licensing and dentistry just to mention a few. For these non-financial cryptocurrencies, the coins are basically tokens used to carry out certain processes in those specific areas. For the purpose of this book, the focus will be limited to the financial cryptocurrencies. Amongst the over 900 cryptocurrencies currently in existence today, there are about 10 that have been uniquely successful and are hugely popular. Some experts in the field prefer to take only 7 of them into consideration (the big 7) but in this book, we will look all 10 of them in some small detail.

The Top 10 Cryptocurrencies

It is common for people to refer to two basic cryptocurrency variants; Bitcoins and Altcoins. Altcoins are all other non-Bitcoin cryptocurrencies. In this context, Bitcoin is given legacy status being the first fully implemented cryptocurrency. Please note that all market capitalization and trading values given for the cryptocurrencies are accurate as of mid-September 2017.

1. Bitcoin (BTC)

Created in 2009 by the anonymous Satoshi Nakamoto, Bitcoin is the most successful of all the other cryptocurrencies, with a market capitalization that stands at over $67 billion. This figure is far greater than all the other cryptocurrencies put together. Such is the popularity and acceptance of bitcoin as a digital currency that a few online merchants have begun to accept payment in bitcoins. Today, there are thousands of bitcoin ATMs all over the world. In terms of nomenclature, Bitcoin, with an Uppercase "B", refers to the Blockchain while bitcoin with a lowercase "b" refers to the currency. The current trading value of Bitcoin is $4,000.

2. Ether (ETH)

Created by Vitalik Buterin in 2014 and launched in mid-2015, Ether is the cryptocurrency for the Ethereum Blockchain. It is the second most popular cryptocurrency after Bitcoin, with a market capitalization of $27 billion which is impressive considering the fact that in September of 2016, an attack on The DAO (Decentralized Autonomous Organization) resulted in a "hard fork" split in the blockchains with two distinct blockchains emerging from it, Ethereum (ETH) and Ethereum Classic (ETC). Ethereum, unlike Bitcoin, is more than just a cryptocurrency. Its use of Smart Contracts running on a Peer-to-Peer network has created the ability to enact contracts without any third-parties. The trading value of Ether is $300.

3. Ripples (XRP)

"Ripples" is the name given to the cryptocurrency for the Ripple Transaction Protocol (RXTP) which is an RTGS (Real-Time Gross Settlement System). It was released in 2012 as part of a collaborative effort between a few developers and Ryan Fugger who created Ripplepay in 2004. It has found a lot of success within mainstream financial institutions where it has been adopted by some in their payment infrastructure technology. It has a market capitalization of $9 billion with a trading value of $0.19

4. Bitcoin Cash (BCH2)

Bitcoin Cash was launched in August of 2017 and in a little over a month, its value has risen astronomically that many investors are beginning to see it as a real contender to Bitcoin for the tag of "most valuable cryptocurrency". Its current market capital capitalization stands at $8 billion which is beyond impressive for a one-month-old cryptocurrency. It also currently trades at about $475. Bitcoin Cash was created as a result of a "hard fork" in the original Bitcoin blockchain due to disagreements centered on the implementation of Bitcoin Improvement Proposal (BIP) 91. This BIP was for the introduction of Segregated Witness (SegWit) which brought up issues relating to maximum block-size limits. As a result, the Bitcoin Cash was implemented by those who were dissatisfied with proceedings and the hard fork was initiated on August 1, 2017. Bitcoin Cash inherited the Bitcoin Blockchain up until the hard fork which happened at block 478558. So, from block

478559, the Bitcoin Cash Blockchain became different from the original Bitcoin Blockchain.

5. Litecoin (LTC)

Litecoin is in many ways similar to bitcoin with the only difference being that transactions proceed faster in Litecoin than in Bitcoin. In fact, the transaction speed is described as "near instant". It was created by Charles Lee and released in October 2011 as an alternative to Bitcoin with a much smaller maximum size blockchain. Most of the other features are the same with bitcoin. It has a market capitalization of $3 billion and a trading value of $55.

6. Dash (DASH)

Lead developer and creator Evan Duffield introduced XCoin in January 2014 which was then changed to "Darkcoin" in February and finally renamed as "Dash" in March of 2015. This final change in nomenclature was to prevent the negative association of the cryptocurrency with the 'dark web'. Dash literally stands for "Digital Cash". It has the same basic features as bitcoins but with much higher transaction speed. It is touted as being the first successful implementation of DAO (Decentralized Autonomous Organization) due to its governance and budgeting framework. Dash has a market capitalization of $2.5 billion and a trading value of $330.

7. NEM (XEM)

NEM stands for New Economy Movement and it is the first ever Smart Asset Blockchain implementation. It was released in March of 2015 after the alpha and beta versions had been tested the previous year. It uses a Proof-of-Importance algorithm to validate transactions rather than the popular Proof-of-work/stake used in most other cryptocurrencies. NEM has a market capitalization of $2.1 billion dollars and it is currently trading at $0.24.

8. IOTA (IOT)

Though still in the open beta testing phase, IOTA has seen some remarkable growth. Created by a group of experts in the blockchain and distributed computing industry, IOTA is one of those cryptocurrencies that have introduced something new and exciting to the cryptocurrency space. IOTA uses a "blockless" distributed ledger (i.e. no transaction blocks linked together in a blockchain). The entire architecture framework looks a lot like a tangled and chaotic mess which is why the technology is called "Tangle" but it is anything but chaotic. Using Directed Acyclic Graph (DAG) as against a traditional blockchain and abandoning the Elliptic Curve Cryptography (ECC) in favor of a much faster hash-based cryptography, transactions in IOTA happen at lightning fast pace making many experts posit that IOTA will be the backbone of the emerging IoT (Internet of Things) technology. IOTA has a market capitalization of $1.6 billion with a trading value of $0.60.

9. Monero (XMR)

Monero was introduced into the cryptocurrency universe in April 2014 as BitMonero (Monero means "coin" in Esperanto). In a way, it's like saying Bitcoin in Esperanto. The name was later shortened to Monero. It is yet another Bitcoin derivative but with a greater emphasis on privacy and improved scalability which is why it even runs on the Android Operating System in addition to the usual suspects; Windows, Mac, and Linux. Transactions in Monero are private, secure and untraceable. Monero is currently valued at $100 with a market capitalization of $1.5 billion.

10. OmiseGo (OMG)

Though yet to be released, OmiseGo is currently the most valued of all the Ethereum-based cryptocurrencies. It is planned for release in the fall or winter of 2017 and will provide a seamless Peer-to-Peer exchange of assets and payments. It has a current exchange value of $10 with a market capitalization of $1 billion.

Ethereum Smart Contract

Technically speaking, for all of the success enjoined by Bitcoin, it does come up a bit short when being applied to anything other than payment processing. As far as utilization of Blockchain Technology goes, this seems a bit like an underutilization. What this means is that while being a truly remarkable payment processing solution devoid of centralized control, Bitcoin doesn't really offer much else in the way of new technology solutions.

It is for this reason that Ethereum is recognized as the of the internet. Think about just how revolutionary Bitcoin the payment processing sphere and apply that to the entire internet. That is what Ethereum is all about. Where Bitcoin has features that limit its applicability, Ethereum, on the other hand, is just a programming language that has infinite possibility. It is as boundless as the internet.

Definition of Smart Contracts

Smart contracts are "self-enforcing" contracts. This means that they do not require a legal system to ensure that terms and conditions are met. The entire functionality of the Ethereum Blockchain is based on Smart Contracts and this is one of the reasons why it has the potential to find application in diverse fields.

In the real world, when two parties enter into a contract, there is a level of oversight required to ensure that terms and conditions are met before consideration (money) is paid or received. In this setting, an arbiter (regulatory body) is required to examine the work done or services provided and deem them to be in line with the contract provisions. This creates a lot of bottlenecks and gives room for disputes.

In the Ethereum Blockchain, there is no need for any of this. The parties entering into a contract merely stipulate inputs coded into the contract transaction. Once these predetermined input conditions are met, the contract is finalized. They work like "if-then" functions in Microsoft Excel; "if" condition A is met, then payment "B" can be released. All of this achieved without any human intervention.

Smart contracts open Blockchain Technology applicability to more aspects of human endeavor than Bitcoin could ever dream. Think about the countless areas that Smart Contracts could be applied to such Vote Counting, Music Licensing, and even Traditional Contracting Processes. The possibilities are limitless.

DAO and DAPP

Apart from smart contracts, Ethereum has also created a lot of potentials for more massive applications to be built. These applications are called Distributed Applications, or "Dapps". Dapps are usually made up of one or more DAOs. DAO stands for Decentralized Autonomous Organization. A DAO is like a long-term contract between many people. Think about a typical organization with support staff, middle management or upper management arranged in a hierarchical order. DAO is just like that but with no centralized controlling body.

In a DAO, prospective members come together to form the DAO each having and exercising voting power in order to make decisions concerning the asset management of the organization. Using a blockchain verified distributed voting mechanism, the members can take decisions on certain matters despite not being in the same geographical location and everyone will trust that there has been no manipulation because of the improved security framework of blockchain technology.

This means that you can have vast Corporations made up of members spread across all corners of the globe. No need for any physical office building as the Corporation exists solely on the blockchain. The potentials are simply limitless. Several DAOs can be grouped together to form vast Integrated Dapps offering a wide spectrum of services.

Bitcoin may have changed the face of global payment processing and paved the way for smarter asset transfer protocols but Ethereum is changing the face of the global internet in ways that make the future a truly exciting prospect to look forward to.

Chapter 3
Investing in Cryptocurrencies

There are those who will say to you that it is too late to profit from the cryptocurrency market. They will say that because you were not an early adopter, you have lost the chance to benefit greatly from investing in the market. These people couldn't be more wrong. The cryptocurrency market is still in its infancy. There are a lot more innovations, progress, growth, and advancements still in the works as far as cryptocurrencies and blockchain technology is concerned. With each passing day, the bar is being pushed even higher and cryptocurrencies are gaining a lot more acceptability in the public sphere.

While it is accurate to posit that cryptocurrencies are the future of money and a wise investment platform, great care must be taken before putting money in the market. Adequate research has to be carried out and you must have a fair understanding of cryptocurrency and blockchain technology. For this reason, a lot of time has been devoted in this book to present the foundational cryptocurrency and blockchain technology knowledge in easy to understand language. The more you understand cryptocurrencies and blockchain technology in general, the more you will be able to make wise decisions when investing in the market.

Cryptocurrency Market Capitalization

As at the time of writing this book, there are over 900 different cryptocurrencies in the market and granted that not all of them have been successful, still, this represents a considerable number. Together, these over 900 different cryptocurrencies have a total market capitalization of $170 billion dollars which represents a massive 850% increase since the start of the year. This is unprecedented in the financial market. There aren't any other tradable assets that have ever experienced such growth. Having read this, you might want to know why all of this is significant. Well, to do that, you must first understand what market capitalization represents.

What is Market Capitalization?

You must have heard of the term market capitalization quite a few times especially when listening to the business news. In simple terms, market capitalization is the monetary value of the outstanding shares of a company. It is a means by which the size of a company can be ascertained. A company can have a small or large "cap" (short for capitalization), depending on the monetary value of its outstanding shares. To determine the market capitalization is actually quite simple and straightforward. It involves multiplying the share price of the company with the total number of outstanding shares.

In the case of Cryptocurrencies, market capitalization is determined by multiplying number the current market value (price) of the coin by the number of coins available. Number of coins available means the number of coins already mined. It does not include all future coin supply numbers. So, for a fictional cryptocoin XYZ, the market capitalization would be determined as follows:

Current price of XYZ coin = $100

Number of available XYZ coins = 5 million

XYZ coin market capitalization = $100 x 5 million = $500 million

The significance of market capitalization data when gauging investments into a cryptocoin is that it provides information on the **"growth versus risk"** analysis. Theoretically speaking, coins with large market cap values tend to experience slower growth but lower risks while the reverse is the case for coins with lower market cap values. Using this as a guide, the safer cryptocoin investments are those that have the largest markets (see Chapter 2: The Top 10 Cryptocurrencies).

Even though the computation for market capitalization seems straightforward, a lot of care must be taken when drawing conclusions from it especially when dealing with some of these obscure Altcoins. Remember that the cryptocurrency market is still young and as such, there is a great deal of manipulation being orchestrated by less than savory characters looking to defraud unsuspecting members of the public.

How to Invest in Cryptocurrency

When it comes to investing in cryptocurrencies, there are three basic activities and these are buying, selling and holding cryptocurrencies. Everything connected to cryptocurrency investment is based on these three activities. At the heart of the matter is the simple principle of **"buying low"** and **"selling high"**. What this simply means is buying coins at a low price and selling at a higher price to make a profit. That is just it, as simple as that but is it really that simple in reality? Well, the truth is an investment in cryptocurrencies can seem daunting to the uninitiated at first, what with the sheer volume of information that must be understood and the high price volatility that seems to be a constant feature of the market. Add to this, the many instances of fraud surrounding some coins on the market and a few people get rightly frightened at getting anywhere near the market.

However, people have made fortunes investing in the cryptocurrency market and not just early adopters only. What is required is the willingness to understand the unique nature of the market and following tried and tested guidelines to help you navigate the cryptocurrency market so that you can make good profits. Just like other forms of investments like stocks and bonds, cryptocurrencies require specific tools for success, without which you cannot hope to adequately take advantage of the market. Before going into the intricacies of trading in cryptocurrencies, there is one crucial aspect of being in the cryptocurrency world that must be attended to. This crucial aspect is, of course, the thing that is known as **cryptocurrency wallets**.

Cryptocurrency Wallets

It can be a bit strange to hear the word "wallet" used in relation to cryptocurrencies, especially when you know that these are virtual coins. Well, just as you can keep your cash and credit cards in wallets so also can you keep your cryptocoins in cryptocurrency wallets.

A cryptocurrency wallet is a term used to describe whatever means is used to store digital coins. Broadly speaking, cryptocurrency wallets fall into two storage categories which are called **"hot storage"** and **"cold storage"**. Hot storage refers to online storage of cryptocoins while cold storage refers to offline storage of cryptocoins. These two storage categories lead to the four different types of cryptocurrency wallets which are discussed briefly below.

Types of Cryptocurrency Wallets

Online Wallets

Online wallets are basically service providers who offer storage of your cryptocoins by simply opening an account with them and depositing your coins. You do this by entering in your details into the appropriate fields when opening your account.

Many consider online wallets to be the least secure of all four types of cryptocurrency wallets and the reasons are very clear. They can easily be compromised by malicious attacks from hackers and they may even suffer data loss from server problems making it difficult to gain access to your coins. The general advice regarding online wallets is that you should only store small amounts of coins on them. Online wallets are a hot storage option.

Paper Wallets

All cryptocoins are secured by means of public and private key cryptography as explained in earlier sections of this book. With paper wallets, all you have to do is print out your public and private key on a piece of paper and that paper automatically becomes a wallet. Paper wallets are a cold storage option.

It is advisable to print backup copies of your paper wallet in case you misplace the main copy. You should also keep your paper wallets safe preferably in safety deposit boxes.

Software Wallets

Software wallets are computer programs that hold cryptocoins. All that is required is downloading the client software and installing same on your computer. The next step is to store the public and private key signatures inside the software program and your coins will automatically become domiciled within the software program.

One drawback with software wallet is the amount of computing space that it requires. Many of the software wallet clients contain the full blockchain of the digital coin thus making them difficult to store on a personal computer. Software wallets are a cold storage option.

Hardware Wallets

A hardware wallet is a USB device within which the public and private key signatures of your cryptocoin can be stored. To use it, you connect the USB device to the computer and follow the prompts from the wallet interface.

Hardware wallets are considered to be the most secure of all the cryptocurrency wallet options. It is also the most expensive of all options. Hardware wallets are a cold storage option.

The Best Wallet Option for Aspiring Cryptocurrency Investors

Generally speaking, all of the wallet options have their own unique advantages and disadvantages. The best wallet is dependent on the specific needs of the person in question. An aspiring cryptocurrency investor is quite different from a cryptocurrency hobbyist. The volume of transactions that will come with being an investor will require a wallet option with robust security features.

A paper wallet would be a poor choice for a cryptocoin investor. This is because using paper wallets require entering the public key and private key signatures or scanning them (you'll need to use QR codes if you intend to scan) when carrying out any transaction. After the transaction is complete, you will need to print a new copy of your paper wallet that reflects the accurate amount of coins in your wallet. Imagine having to do this on multiple occasions in a single day.

Online wallets are susceptible to malicious cyber-attacks from hackers. Many of the service providers of online cryptocoin wallets do not have the online infrastructure to guard against intrusions from hackers. Even the most secure sites get hacked from time to time so it is no surprise that online cryptocurrency wallets get targeted all the time too.

Software wallets while being a cold storage option can still be affected by malware which can cause the software to fail. If you have not backed up your account offline on your computer, then such malware attacks can make you lose valuable coins.

Hardware wallets are portable and secure. They also have additional layers of security not present in any other wallet option. If you are serious about investing in cryptocurrencies, then having a hardware wallet is the way to go. They are a lot more expensive than all the other options, usually costing somewhere between $50 and $200. Considering all the security, portability and easy backup options provided by hardware wallets, the price is definitely a minor inconvenience.

If you wish to get hardware wallet as an aspiring cryptocurrency investor, there are a number of brands open to you such as **Trezor** and **Ledger Nano S**. These two brands are the touted as the undisputed kings of the cryptocurrency hardware wallet scene and are recommended for people who want to participate in cryptocurrency investment due to the many security features on offer by the pair of them.

How to Invest in Cryptocurrencies

Cryptocurrency trading includes the same basic activities as with other tradable assets. There is buying, selling and holding. The aim is usually to make a profit by buying at lower prices and selling at much higher prices. In order to trade cryptocurrencies, there two essential tools that you must have and they are a cryptocurrency wallet and a cryptocurrency exchange platform. Cryptocurrency exchange platforms are websites where you can perform cryptocurrency trading operations i.e. buying, selling and exchanging one cryptocurrency for another cryptocurrency. Cryptocurrency exchange platforms even allow you exchange cryptocoins for fiat currency like USD, GBP, EUR, AUD etc.

There are organizations that function like a hybrid wallet-exchange meaning that they provide both wallet and exchange services. A good example of such an organization is Coinbase. Most of these organizations provide the option of direct trading and investments on the platform making the entire process a lot easier, like a one-stop hub for all your cryptocurrency investment activities. One disadvantage of Coinbase is that you can only trade Bitcoin, Ethereum, and Litecoin on the platform. So, if you wish to trade other coins, you will need a second cryptocurrency exchange. There are a number of options to choose from such as Kraken, GDAX, and Bittrex.

If you are new to the cryptocurrency investment scene, it is perhaps wiser to use Coinbase (if you are American) or any other reputable wallet-exchange hybrid company so as to keep things simple. When you begin to get the hang of the process, you can diversify your portfolio to include other exchanges that offer other cryptocoins. Even if you are an expert trader in stocks and bonds, cryptocurrencies are a different matter entirely so it is best to start small.

Using Coinbase as an example, the following are the steps that will be taken when trading cryptocurrencies.

Step One

You will have to sign up with Coinbase by visiting their website. You open an account with Coinbase and your journey begins. You have the option of using their wallet service or choosing to use your own hardware wallet. Using your own hardware wallet is highly recommended.

Step Two

The second step involves selecting your payment method. Coinbase offers numerous payment methods such as bank account, debit card, and credit card. This makes exchanging cryptocoin for your local currency and vice-versa a lot easier. Be sure to take a look at the fees for each payment option before deciding on the one to use. Also, pay attention to the approval time interval i.e. how long it will take for your payments to be approved.

Step Three

Once your payment method is approved, you can begin to buy cryptocurrencies. On Coinbase you can buy Bitcoin, Ethereum, and Litecoin. Once you buy your first cryptocoins, the trading process commences where you make decisions on when to sell, exchange, or hold. As you progressively get better at trading, you will want to sign up with another exchange platform and begin to perform exchanges between different cryptocurrencies.

A few things to keep in mind

1. Volatility.

   Cryptocurrencies are highly volatile. The market experiences incredible fluctuations in prices and as such great care must be taken when making decisions based on current market value.

2. Adequate Research.

   Bitcoin, Ethereum, and Litecoin have experienced some form of growth and stability in the past few months. New cryptocoin offerings are notorious for sprouting almost every day boasting unrealistic benefits. Before investing in any of these new cryptocurrencies, be sure to do adequate research. Don't be hesitant to rely on expert opinions but be sure that you are following unbiased experts like can be found on Coincap and Blockfolio.

3. Government Regulation.

In many countries, there isn't really a well-defined legal policy on cryptocurrencies. Some countries are friendly towards it while others are downright hostile with a few not coming out to promote or clampdown on cryptocurrencies. It is a good idea to get an understanding of the position of the government in your country when it comes to cryptocurrencies so as not to run afoul of the law and lose your investments in the process.

Chapter 4
Mining Cryptocurrencies

You have probably come across the term cryptocurrency mining before on the pages of websites and blogs or perhaps from a friend or relative trying to get you interested in cryptocurrencies. Mining is an essential aspect of any cryptocurrency operation as it is the process by which transactions are validated and new "coins" created. For those who might be wondering why the term "mining", when a transaction is verified and added to the blockchain, new coins are In this chapter, particular attention will be paid to mining Bitcoin and Ethereum with a brief description given for other Altcoins.

Definition

Cryptocurrency mining can be defined simply as the process by which transactions are authenticated and added to the public distributed ledger on the blockchain. The node responsible for successfully validating the transaction block is rewarded with a specified number of coins. This is how new coins are created in the Bitcoin blockchain as well as other cryptocurrencies that follow the same protocol.

Bitcoin Mining

Bitcoin is a financial ecosystem where transactions are carried out when bitcoins are transferred from one address to another as a means of exchanging value. Remember that Bitcoin is the blockchain and bitcoin is the cryptocurrency. For any currency to have value, it must be scarce. This is why Governments and their respective Central Banks maintain strict control over the liquidity levels, i.e. the amount of currency in circulation. If we all just started printing Dollar, Pounds, Euro, Yen and all the other currency notes in our basements, these currencies would have no value whatsoever. The same principle applies to the Bitcoin Blockchain where if anyone could just assign XYZ amount of bitcoins to themselves, then bitcoins would have absolutely no value.

Breaking Down the Basics of Bitcoin Mining

If you were to perform a simple search for the keywords: "Bitcoin Mining" on any internet search engine, you would see results that convey information similar to the sentence below:

"Bitcoin Mining is the process by which transactions on the Bitcoin network are verified and added to the public distributed blockchain ledger and also the means by which new bitcoins are created."

From this definition, it is clear that Bitcoin Mining achieves two things: verifying transactions and creating new coins. The main mining process is all about verifying transactions and adding them as transactions blocks thus continuing the blockchain. The creation of new coins is a form of reward for the mining node that is successfully able to verify the transaction first.

To the bitcoin neophyte, you may think what's to stop someone from creating fake transactions, verifying them and obtaining the rewards? Well, the following is a concise explanation of why that is not possible. Great care will be taken to break down all technical terms so as to make for easy reading.

The Role of Bitcoin Miners

The Bitcoin Mining process is extremely complex. It involves having to solve a difficult mathematical puzzle in order to add a block to the blockchain. This process of solving the mathematical puzzle is what is called the **"Proof-of-Work" (POW)**. The proof-of-work while being easy for others to verify once obtained, is extremely difficult to solve. The difficulty in finding the solution for the proof-of-work is what ensures the fidelity of the mining process while the ease of verifying the proof-of-work is what enables fast transaction times in Bitcoin. Imagine if it took ages for others to agree that a block has been mined, transactions would take such a long to be verified and Bitcoin would not be as popular as it is today.

The Bitcoin Mining Process

The process begins with the identification of transactions and ends with the reward of a certain number of bitcoins to the miner (more specifically, the mining node) that was able to identify and verify a transaction before any other mining node. The process is best explained using a stepwise approach as detailed in the following steps:

- Step One

    Mining nodes crawl through the vast Bitcoin Blockchain Network searching for transactions. Within the Bitcoin

Blockchain, there are transactions being carried out like payment for products online, subscribing for online gaming platforms etc. These transactions are floating around in something called the **memory pool**. These transactions in the memory all have a different status. Some of them are invalid for one reason or the other, others have already been mined and are awaiting authentication while there are some that are valid but yet to be mined. Mining nodes scour the memory pool searching for the latter type of transactions.

- Step Two

Mining nodes will eventually find yet to be mined transactions in the memory pool. These transactions will then be put together inside something called a **candidate block**. Candidate blocks are not part of the blockchain. They only exist within the environment of the mining node, sort of like a notepad where a reporter scribbles down points while pursuing a story. Once these transactions are put into a candidate block, the mining process begins.

Before moving to step three, it is important to point out a vital piece of information which will provide context for a better understanding of the subsequent steps. The mining process is a competitive one. This means that mining nodes are in competition with each other to identify unconfirmed transactions, aggregating them into a candidate block and finding the proof-of-work solution. This competitive mining within bitcoin is known as the **hashing race**.

- Step Three

    Mining nodes utilize hashing to arrive at a solution which will validate the transactions in the candidate block. Each candidate block has a header. Mining nodes calculate the hash of this header in order to come up with a value that is less than the value of the specific target. These mining nodes use a specific hashing function called the **SHA256** function. The name SHA256 stems from the fact that regardless of the input size, the size of the output value is **always** 256bits.

    If the output value obtained isn't less than the required target, the mining node carries out another hash in order to come up with a different solution. This process will be repeated several times until a solution for the header that is lower than the expected value is found. This repetitive hashing process involves using various **"nonce values"** until an appropriate solution which constitutes a proof-of-work is found.

- Step Four

    After a mining node has successfully found a solution to the candidate block header that is lower than the specific target, the **"mined block"** is the broadcasted to the other nodes in the Bitcoin Blockchain so that validation of the proof-of-work can commence. If there is a majority consensus, i.e. 51 percent of the network agrees with the proof-of-work solution, the mined candidate block becomes a **"verified block"**. The verified block is added to the blockchain which updates automatically across the network so that all nodes running the full blockchain will have the newly added transaction block.

- Step Five

Once the mined block becomes a verified transaction block, other mining nodes abandon their attempts at solving the proof-of-work for the candidate block and go in search for new unconfirmed transactions in the memory pool. The final step of the Bitcoin mining process is the award of bitcoins to the successful mining node. As of 2017, the reward for successfully mining bitcoins is 12.5btc per block.

Advancements in Bitcoin Mining

Mining bitcoins is one of the ways in which a person can acquire bitcoins. Based on this, the number of mining nodes in the Bitcoin Blockchain Network has continued to increase. Miners wish to take advantage of the block reward as well as the fees they are entitled to when verifying transactions. With the proliferation of miners on the network, there has been a lot of advancement in mining technology over the years. In this section, the changes that have occurred in terms of mining hardware on the Bitcoin Blockchain will be discussed briefly.

Back in 2008 and 2009 when Bitcoin was still in its infancy, you could mine bitcoins with just your regular laptops or desktops. The CPUs (Central Processing Units) of your common office or household computer was able to perform the hashing operation in order to provide the proof-of-work solution to the candidate block header. The typical hashing speed was around about 8MH/sec (8 megahashes per second) i.e. 8 million hashes per second. This was within the hardware capabilities of most CPUs. The reason for this was due to the fact that the Bitcoin Network had few nodes and the blockchain was nowhere near as long as it is today. The process of finding unconfirmed transactions in the memory pool didn't take long.

By 2010, Bitcoin was becoming more popular and people were beginning to become interested in the network. Mining has always been a competitive race, so it was only natural that some folks would seek for ways to give themselves a competitive edge over others. This led to the switch from CPU to GPU (Graphics Processing Unit). GPUs afforded miners more hashing power with an average hashing speed of 110MH/sec, an increase of over 1000 percent. What this means was miners running GPUs were 1000 times faster and 1000 times more likely to complete a mining operation than anyone still running the Bitcoin client on a normal CPU.

Buoyed by the improvements in mining technology, the Bitcoin Network grew even more and by the year 2011, there was a massive departure from processing units to even more advanced mining hardware setups known as FPGA (Field Programmable Gate Arrays). FPGAs took Bitcoin mining to stratospheric heights and led the way to the increase in the value of bitcoins. This also marked the beginning of the end for single mining operations with the introduction of integrated mining setups that utilized multiple mining hardware all synchronized to produce improved mining performance. The hashing speed also increased tremendously to an average of about 7TH/sec (7 terahashes per second) i.e. 7 trillion hashes per second, an increase of over 6,000,000 percent. What this means was miners running FPGAs were 6 million times faster and more likely to complete a mining operation than anyone running the Bitcoin client on a GPU.

In 2013, it became apparent that there was the need to create fully specialized hardware dedicated solely to mining bitcoins. This culminated in the creation of ASIC (Application Specific Integrated Circuit) mining hardware. ASIC mining hardware allowed for SHA256 hashing process to be run directly on state of the art silicon chips designed specifically to mine bitcoins. The results were and have been astonishing. It is the system that is still in use today and it shows no sign of slowing down. With ASICs, average hashing speed now stands at 100PH/sec (100 petahashes per second) i.e. 100 quadrillion hashes per second, an increase of more than 1,000,000 percent. What this means is that miners running ASIC are a million times faster than miners running FPGAs.

In order to understand just how powerful ASICs are, one ASIC hardware unit provides more hashing power today than the entire Bitcoin network had in 2010! Just think about that for a second and realize how much progress has been made. As a consequence of the increased hashing power, the level of difficulty encountered during the mining process has also risen tremendously. This is to be expected otherwise, the mining process would lose all fidelity and bitcoin will cease to have any value. Experts who have studied Bitcoin over the years have stated that in the year 2017, it became 20 billion times more difficult to mine bitcoins than in 2009. 20 billion percent increase in difficulty in 8 years tells a remarkable story.

How to get involved in Bitcoin Mining

Back in 2008/2009, you could join the world of bitcoin mining with a laptop and be able to mine a few coins. These days, the odds of a miner using a laptop being able to successfully mine bitcoin are theoretically zero. With the upsurge in the sheer number of mining nodes and the improvements in mining hardware, it has become a popular practice for miners to band together into what is known as a **"mining pool"**. Miners come together to form these mining pools in a bid to improve the odds of being able to successfully mine bitcoins. Anyone serious about getting into the bitcoin mining arena in this present time has to join a mining pool if they are to stand any chance of ever being able to mine bitcoins.

What is a Mining Pool?

A mining pool is simply a collection of mining nodes that have been combined into one super giant node. The hashing power of each individual mining node in the pool is brought together creating an integrated mining node capable of performing hashes at incredible speeds.

There are two basic types of mining pools and these are the traditional mining pool and the P2Pool. Both have their merits and demerits but they offer better chances of being able to mine bitcoins than mining solo.

Factors to consider when choosing a mining pool

When something becomes as popular as bitcoin, there is always the danger of falling victim to fraudulent individuals seeking to make money with scams of different varieties. While there are genuine mining pools, there are also a great many fake mining pools being advertised on the internet. Most of these fake pools are basically Ponzi schemes. As a result, great care should be taken when choosing a mining pool to join.

There are a number of factors that one must consider when joining a mining pool. Perhaps the most important are the size of the mining pool and the mining pool account type.

A large-sized mining pool means greater odds of being able to successfully mine a block and clam the block reward. This is due to the increased hashing power of large-sized mining pools. The downside here is that due to a large number of participants in the mining pool, the payouts will be small. A small sized mining pool will have a comparatively larger payout but the odds of successfully mining bitcoin are materially diminished.

There are two types of mining pool accounts: the local mining account and the cloud mining account. In local mining, the miner connects his/her mining hardware to the mining pool and becomes part of the mining pool network. In the case of cloud mining, no hardware is required. A prospective miner simply enters into an online mining contract with a cloud mining service and receives earnings. Local miners on the average earn more than cloud miners. Many cloud mining services have also been found to be internet scams.

Ethereum Mining

The Ethereum cryptocurrency is known as "Ether" (ETH). Ether is the second most popular and valuable cryptocurrency after Bitcoin. Ethereum shares some similarities with the Bitcoin Network in the sense that it is also a decentralized blockchain that uses proof-of-work transaction verification. While Bitcoin only really finds application in payment processing, Ethereum has almost universal applicability especially with its use of Smart Contracts. For this reason, it has always been important for developers on the Ethereum Network to ensure that entry-level miners didn't face trouble becoming miners with expensive mining hardware requirements like the way it is on Bitcoin.

In order to make this a reality, the Casper Proof of Stake algorithm was implemented which basically rendered ASICs useless. Remember that in the previous section of this chapter, ASICs were shown to be the mining powerhouse for Bitcoins. The Casper Proof of Stake algorithm essentially limited Ethereum mining to GPUs. What this means is that you don't necessarily need to make a huge financial investment into ASIC units in order to mine Ether. It must be stated here that even with these measures, it hasn't completely eradicated the issue of highly centralized mining setups that have effectively overtaken the market. Investors have simply massed multiple GPUs together and used the collective mining power of such assemblies to control the mining process.

The Ethereum Mining Algorithm

Prior to 2016, Proof-of-work was the mining algorithm used on Ethereum and the process mirrored that of Bitcoin quite closely. After 2016, when the switch was made to the Casper Proof of Stake algorithm, a lot of things changed in Ethereum mining. It became a lot easier to validate transactions and the time lag reduced tremendously. It has always been clear to many Cryptocurrency and Blockchain experts that Proof-of-Work was fundamentally flawed in some ways and a better transaction verification system was needed, one that vastly improved speed and reduced energy consumption in the process. Casper is just one of the successful implementations of this paradigm shift in the Blockchain sphere.

How to Get Involved Ethereum Mining

Even though there have been concerted efforts to ensure that entry cost into Ethereum mining is kept at a minimum, it would not necessarily be a wise idea to try and start mining Ether on your own. Just like in the Bitcoin Network, joining a pool of miners is still the better option. There are two main options for anyone wishing to explore this option and these options are Ethereum Mining Pools and Ethereum Cloud Mining.

In Ethereum Mining Pools, miners join with a network of other miners thus increasing their probability of being able to acquire Ether by successfully validating transaction blocks. There are many Ethereum Mining Pool configurations adopted by several Ethereum Mining Pools. Most of these configurations are based on the method used to distribute revenue within the network. The most popular configurations are Proportional Payouts (PROP) and Pay per Share (PPS). In recent times, there has also been a new configuration that is becoming increasingly popular and it called the Double Geometric Method (DGM).

Ethereum Cloud Mining is a lot like Bitcoin Cloud Mining in the sense that it involves entering into a mining contract with a Cloud Mining service provider. There are various forms of Ethereum Cloud Mining and they include Virtual Hosted Mining, Leased Hashing Power and Hosted Mining Services. As is the case with Bitcoin, some Ethereum Cloud Mining service providers are actually internet scams.

Conclusion

Thank you for purchasing this book and taking the time to read its contents thoroughly. A lot of effort has been put into making sure the language of the book is clear and concise so that readers can easily understand the more technical aspects of the subject matter.

By completing the beginners' guide, you should now have a good understanding of Blockchain Technology, Cryptocurrency Investment, and Cryptocurrency Mining. It is hoped that all the information contained within this book has added value to you, the reader.

If you enjoyed this book as much as I've enjoyed writing it, you can subscribe* to my email list for exclusive content and sneak peaks of my future books.

Click the link below:
http://eepurl.com/du_qcj

OR

Use the QR Code:

(*Must be 13 years or older to subscribe)

Conclusion

Printed in Great Britain
by Amazon